"With Love, *Always*"

"With Love, *Always*"

A Tool Box For Life Series

Annette Renaud

To order additional copies of this book, contact:
Xlibris Corporation
1-888-795-4274
www.Xlibris.com
Orders@Xlibris.com
79163

Contents

Tool One   Laughter is the best medicine. 13

Tool Two   We are given one mouth and two ears. 17

Tool Three   Balancing Act 21

Tool Four   Lead and Others will Follow.................................25

Tool Five   Believe it, baby! 29

Tool Six   Turn it on!...33

Tool Seven   Knowledge is Power 37

Tool Eight   To Forgive is to Divine 41

Tool Nine   " . . . Wisdom perfects a person's speculative reason
                in matters of judgement about the truth."
                (Thomas Aquinas)...45

Tool Ten   "If I only had courage."
                (said the Cowardly Lion in the *Wizard of Oz*)...................49

Tool Eleven   "I think I can, I think I can."
                ('The Little Engine That Could') 53

Tool Twelve   Step Three: Make a decision to turn our will
                and our lives over to the care of God
                as we understood Him.......................................57

Further Tidbits of Wisdom...59

To my children:
Shannon, Danielle, Megan, Sara, John, Steven, Catherine,
Virginia and Karoline
Thank you for teaching me, I love you very much

To my husband, Larry, for originating this inspirational idea
To Mom and Dad, Thank YOU for loving me so well!

My Dear Child,

I know you do not like being called a child. You are an adult now, growing stronger every day. Yet, you have come from my womb so I still see you as the baby that I took home from the hospital. I am not sure if that is a good thing or a bad thing; it just is. That day changed my life forever. I no longer worried about where I was going to eat, I was worried if I was going to be able to feed you. You were my world as I was your world. As time marched on and your world expanded, mine did too. You see, my child, I had to force my world to become smaller so that I was able to see the world through your eyes. You know something? It scared me to become smaller. But to become smaller has actually expanded my own world and perceptions of it. I was changed forever.

As you learned to do things for yourself and I was trying to figure out what it meant to be a mother, gifts were imparted both ways. Even as a powerless child, you gave me wisdom and other gifts for my own heart. At the same time, my gifts were being imparted to you.

I know that you could write your own book on every life and parental mistake I made. I know that I could probably write one too! "The do's and don'ts of life and being a parent" . . . I think that is what I would call it. It sure would be a big book! As I look back at my own humanity, I wish I could have spared you so much.

I also know that, at the same time, some great tools were handed down into your own heart and mind as you grew into the young person that you are! Please do not be insulted if I call you 'young'. Remember, anyone under the age of 35 is young to me! I am smiling as I write this to you, my child. I am thankful for the opportunity to share with you my own journey into my own growth and that your life and my life are intertwined.

This book is my gift to you. It is a lifetime condensed into a few pages between a front and a back cover. Upon reflection over the years, I realized that there were some incredible gifts, or should I call them life tools, that were handed down to you. Through life's lessons of joy and sorrow, these tools have come to you wrapped with Faith.

I am going to list some of the tools that I have imparted to you. As you read them, know that I know that you will be gaining even more as you surpass me in tools. It is time for me to fade and you to shine. You are young and full of so many promises. Go realize them; go earn your own stripes in this world; go gain your own wisdom and faith; and go collect even more tools to pass on to the next generation.

I want to thank you for the journey. It has been a pleasure having you as part of my walk on this earth. There is not one thing that I would change. If I did change one part of my own history, chances are you as you would not have existed. What a sad place this world would be without you. You bring it such flavor!

I hope you are not uncomfortable that I am writing you a book of love. It comes from my heart. I love you, my child. No matter where you are, how old you are or where I am . . . that love will always be present. It is there to lend strength to your life as you make your own way.

I love you.

Can you believe it? You have come of age before my very eyes. I am so grateful for the time spent with you. As you are now older our time together is lessening. You are spreading your own wings now. You have been groomed for this moment, my child. You are ready. You are able. You are strong and beautiful.

Laughter is the best medicine.

Tool One

Laughter is the best medicine.

This tool is so key. It is the tool of all tools! It is the one that will allow the flood of all other tools to enter and be learned. It is the tool that brings joy and laughter as you walk your journey on this earth. I have hoped, over the years, as we have addressed good times and challenging times, that this tool came forth loud and clear. It is the tool of a *sense of humor.*

I have chosen this tool to be number one. You ask yourself, "Why? What a goofy tool to choose as number ONE." Yep, it sure is! I am in agreement with you on this.

Over the course of sharing our lives together, sense of humor has come in handy as we learned how to love each other. It was reached for in moments of stress, discomfort, fear, anger, sadness, crisis, and celebration. Sense of humor was taken out of my toolbox when those particular moments rose up. I knew that when sense of humor came forth it would crack the oppressive moments turning them into moments of victory and lessons. It also added such a great flavor to our celebrations! We would laugh so hard!

Your life, as you break from me, will be filled with so many different situations. All of these situations can be opportunities to grow further in character, life, and faith. Sense of humor enables the challenging situations that will arise to be more palatable and easier to swallow.

Honey, everyone you meet is in the middle of a humbling life lesson. That is one of the greatest truths about humanity. You are not alone. What separates people is how they deal with their lessons. This tool enables you to deal with your life lessons with a bit more class and bit more love.

Sense of humor allows you to laugh, not only at the circumstances, but also at yourself as you learn more and more about who you are, what you stand for within your own soul and those around you. It is such a powerful tool. It can bring joy to your life and those around you. It can teach you how to treat yourself as you walk your own personal and private journey. Life was not meant to be taken all that seriously, just serious enough to be accountable, yet light enough to smell the roses on your way to wisdom.

You see, my child, many people realize that in reaching goals in life they have to get serious; that the pursuit of happiness is just that, a pursuit. The search is a definite challenge, yet one where all of us are asked to step up to that proverbial plate and swing our own bats. Do it with a smile on your face! Smile, love, laugh and enjoy the journey, my child. It is your own eternal gift; your life. Enjoy the long walk!

We are given one mouth and two ears.

Tool Two

We are given one mouth and two ears.

The ***tool of listening*** is so important. Wars between nations have occurred because of the lack of this tool. Battles within families take place because listening is not taken seriously.

As the old adage says, "We are given one mouth and two ears because we are to listen twice as much as we speak." Over the years this is something that we have had to work on many times. I know that I tend to get on that soapbox, that parents step on, and talk and talk and talk. As a result, misunderstandings between us have grown disproportionately. Boy, if I put a quarter in a box every time I spoke before listening, I could have been rich!

I can recall moments where the listening was perfect and I heard you. I heard your pain, joy, sadness, confidence, fear, laughter and so many other emotions as you shared your thoughts. At those moments, I was so grateful that I was able to 'get it right.'

As you learn to listen and practice listening you will find that people have a lot to say. Even in 'small' relationships, such as you and someone special, you will be much more successful for having listened closely and really hear what the other person is saying. You tend to notice the little things about the person and what they are trying to convey to you. Sometimes what someone is saying is not what is going on in their hearts. You will be able to 'hear' the heart tell its tale through the sharing of another person.

I chose the word 'small' because one on one is as basic and little as you can get. It is not small because of its lack of importance. It will become a number one priority through the choice of being with one special person as a life partner. Your own personal power will grow as you nurture the tool of listening in this particular relationship. It will expand into all facets of your life, enriching it to the point of pure peace.

We have shared the same joys, sorrows, challenges, and laughter. In all of it, I am constantly being challenged to grow as a listener. It never ends because you are an adult. It just begins as you grow up and leave. It is the beginning of an amazing journey into a life full of character.

There were times, as a parent, that I did not take the time to listen to you and your own sharing. It seems as though, at times, my own issues seemed to block the sharing between us. I will continue my own journey as you continue yours working on this awesome tool. I work on it so that I can grow more into the parent that you need and deserve. Even though you are growing up and our time is limited now, I will always be the parent in this relationship of ours, this great dance of family. You will also work on it as you grow in your own identity as a person, employee, employer, lover, friend, sibling and son or daughter. Isn't life just grand? It is full of so many surprises and so many wonderful experiences of growth.

Let us move on! You know how mushy I can get as I express my feelings! I will be repeating to you how proud I am of who you are and what you are striving to become.

Balancing Act

Tool Three

Balancing Act

Wow, this tool is a challenge! It is the ***tool of balancing***. The expectations for you as an adult will always be one of challenge as God has called all people to be upright. Becoming an upright adult is the quest of all adults. In our search for Truth, love, and peace, we prayerfully try to bring some sense of order into our own lives. As you have watched me over the years, you have witnessed me working, cooking, loving, living, advocating, volunteering for political organizations, picketing, praying, and laying around in the total luxury of being occasionally lazy.

As an adult, you will be called upon to pray for your own family, provide for your family, stand for justice, pursue your own dreams, live a life of personal growth as you heal and live at the same time. You will be called upon to be the life partner of someone precious to you. It is much, and yet it is light when you do it with balance.

Surrendering the pull on your time to a natural flow leaves the door open for so many opportunities to come your way. It has taken me many years to figure out that we have very little control over our lives. It is funny. As I have grown, I have begun to sense something bigger than myself at work in my life. It is like taking a plunge into the deep rushing waters of life and allowing yourself to be propelled by the stream of grace as it moves within your life.

Let go, my child. Let your gifts shine through! Your gifts are many! The gifts want to be expressed and they want out of you. Only you can bring them out. No one else has them and no one else can express them like you can. Find the balance in your life and find yourself.

I believe in you. In your search you will find your own niche in this world and be important to many people. It all began with you being important to just one person . . . and that was me. Now that you have grown you have become important to many and that importance will continue to grow.

Lead and Others will Follow

Tool Four

Lead and Others will Follow

As you have heard many times, "when much is given, much is expected." This tool is the ***tool of leadership***. This tool will serve you incredibly well throughout your life. You will need it often. You will be in situations where you will be the lone voice of reason, you will be in situations that will demand a person to stand for justice and what is right. You will know what to do. When you have used this tool correctly, in the past, I have been very proud of you.

Being a leader is not being the loudest voice, nor is it being the strongest. A leader is one who can forge through paths that are not taken by the many; a path taken by few. As you take this path, all on the other beaten down path will look to see how to join you.

As I have watched you grow into a young adult, I have been privy to many rebellious moments as you shed the child and gained in adult stature. That growth is, by no means, an easy feat in today's world. Navigating the onslaught of so much societal chaos as well as 'pop' peer pressure is like trying to walk through a minefield unscathed.

Sometimes I think your rebellion was about your heart responding to all of the injustices that went on around you. It was your way of expressing the wrongness of it all.

It is important to build on your strengths and do what is right even if it is something you don't want to do. As you exercise this tool, it will grow into something incredibly empowering. Cultivate it with sensitivity, and you will lead others instead of them leading you.

Believe it, baby!

Tool Five

Believe it, baby!

Yea, baby, confidence, confidence, confidence, confidence! The ***tool of believing in yourself*** will carry you in many situations. This is a tool I am still working on myself. I bring it out at the oddest of times and yet, when it would be strategic, I don't even take it out of my toolbox!

Believe in your abilities! Believe in your gifts! Believe in your talents! Believe in your looks! Believe in your intelligence! Believe that you are loved and worthy of being loved! What makes that apparently homely guy get "the girl"? His confidence! What makes an athlete shut out the crowd and sink the winning basket with no time left on the clock? His/Her confidence! What makes others believe in you and trust what you say? Confidence! It is so much easier to believe the negative messages we tell ourselves; that we are not loved, we are stupid and can't do anything right. It is so much easier to become our own obstacle then it is to believe the inherent truth of our very being. WE ARE AWESOME.

As the saying goes, God is not in the business of making junk. He never has nor will he ever make junk. He stated as he sat back and looked at what He created, "It is good." If anything but glowing words come into your head they are not from God. They are from old paradigms that come from negative experiences. We all got 'em and we all struggle with either turning them into gold or letting them lead us to mediocrity.

It is time to say GOODBYE to those pests! It is time to truly believe in what we are about and where we are going. It is time to turn from the past and look toward the life of tomorrow. Yea! Believe in yourself! I do! You are something very special.

Throughout our time together, I hope you have witnessed me taking this tool out, brushing it off, and instilling it into my life more and more as I have matured. Not only do I use it for myself but in doing so I show you how to use it proactively in your life. You will now carry it in your toolbox and bring it to fruition. Always remember, the more you do, the better you feel, the better you feel, the more you believe, and the more you believe, the more you become. Go get 'em, tiger!

Turn it on!

Tool Six

Turn it on!

This is a cool one. It is the ***tool of love and passion***, sometimes known as a big heart. This you have in abundance. Most people think of this tool as being used just for one special person in life and, of course, your family. Nope, that is not the case. This is about using love and passion for what life throws at you. (And, boy, sometimes life throws huge curve balls when you least expect it!) What makes someone of equal intelligence learn faster? It is a love and a passion for learning. What makes an average basketball player grow to be great? It is a passion for the game. What makes one relationship stand out as special? It is a love and a passion for another human being. What makes one singer stand out of a group? It is a love of music and an ability to express passion. What makes one person stand out from others? Is it a passion for imparting truth, love and an interest in the passions of life? Is it the interest in a job well done? Can you see yourself? We are watching you grow such an incredible passion for the life that you are developing. We are proud of you. This is the answer to all boredom . . . actively choosing to love and embrace all situations! Allow yourself to love as much as possible. Approach life with passion!

We hope, through our own choices and actions that we have displayed this tool. We are grateful for so many things and love with great passion. At times, we falter from our ideal, yet we still pick ourselves up, brush ourselves off, and get back into the business of life with gusto, love, passion and hugs.

I love the words in a speech by Theodore Roosevelt, "The Man in the Arena":

> *"It is not the critic who counts; not the man (or woman) who points out how the strong man (or woman) tumbles, or where the doer of deeds could have done them better. The credit belongs to the man (or woman) who is actually in the arena, whose face is marred by dust and sweat and blood; who strives valiantly; who errs, who comes short again and again, because there is no effort without error and shortcoming; but who does actually strive to do the deeds; who knows great enthusiasms, the great devotions; who spends himself (or herself) in a worthy cause; who at the best knows in the end the triumph of high achievement, and who at the worst, if he (or she) fails, at least fails while daring greatly, so that his (her) place shall never be with those cold and timid souls who neither know victory nor defeat."*

Roosevelt shows us what passion can do in a person's life. When you have passion it brings you face to face with who you are and what you are. Without it, life has very little purpose or meaning except to 'just get by', accepting the status quo. Well, my child, America was not built by people who just wanted to get by. It was built by those who believed in something bigger than themselves. These men and women had a passion for freedom that was only a concept at that time. We, as a people, are reaping the benefits of a past passion: the passion for a future of freedoms never before experienced by a body of people. To this day there is no other country with such ideals. It will take that same passion to keep it in place for future generations.

Now, I have a trivia question for you. Who was Theodore Roosevelt? If you can't remember, it is time to get back into that toolbox of yours and reach for the next tool . . . .

Knowledge is Power

Tool Seven

Knowledge is Power

Knowledge is such a powerful tool. When you were a child first learning how to read, it was so exciting to watch your early attempts at grasping the seeds of learning how to obtain knowledge. I adored watching you grow up to be the wonderful person that you are today. I count it a blessing and a privilege to be part of the seedling growth as you took your first rudimentary steps towards accumulating knowledge.

There have been times when I have watched you struggle to gain even a little knowledge. Then there were times where your use of the tool passion transformed you into a bottomless pit of information about something! It was exciting to watch you find out, through trial and error, how to gain knowledge.

You have watched me read, read and do more reading. You have seen all kinds of books rest in my hands as I devoured the pages. You have seen self-help, spiritual, theological, philosophical, nonfiction, fiction, science fiction, historical and romance be caressed lovingly as I read, and reread some. The knowledge that I have gained from just reading books is empowering. My hope is that as my life experiences deepen my character, knowledge will bring wisdom that will top off the sundae of my own growth. In so doing, it can be shared with your own budding knowledge as you gain your own experiences, knowledge and wisdom. What else is family for if not for the giving, sharing and the partaking of the bountiful blessings that we can offer each other?

Ahhhhhh, this now leads me to the next tool . . . .

To Forgive is to Divine

Tool Eight

To Forgive is to Divine

This one is one of the toughest to pull out of that darn toolbox. It is one of the heaviest tools in there so that it is hard to get it out and use it. Trust me! I have seen grown men and women not even bother to try. It is (drum roll please . . .) the ***tool of Forgiveness***. How do I know about the difficulty of applying this tool? I struggle with it every day, my child. Say the word, "forgiveness." It sounds like a soft and fuzzy word, doesn't it? In just saying the word, you feel a sense of peace inside yourself. Yet, using it is another thing entirely.

As you grow into a wise adult, you will be able to see my frailties, faults, and failings. I call that the three "f s' of humanity! Boy, do I have many! I could even write them all down just to help shorten the enlightening process that you will be undertaking as you undo some of my mistakes in your own life! It will take place. Even in the most perfect of circumstances the circumstance is not perfect. That is why this tool will be so very important. Our lives are meant to be interwoven with other lives. Because we are not perfect, nor is anyone we encounter, we will love and be loved imperfectly. Some people won't even bother loving they will just take. We will be disavowed, abused, disappointed, shamed, embarrassed and hurt. We can't get around it. No matter how many policies, laws or controls, we are not going to change the fact that bad stuff will happen to us in our lifetime.

What separates people is the choices that they make when looking at the construction of such circumstances. People can let the hurts keep heaping up one on top of another. If that is the case, over the years a tall wall will be built. No one will be able to get over it and you will not be able to get over it. You will be trapped inside with all of the hurt, disillusionment, resentment, and anger. It will rule your every thought and determine how you manage your own relationships and life.

It took me years to figure this one out. I still struggle with pulling the tool of forgiveness out. Wrongs were done to me at times. At least that is how I perceived the situations. What I have learned is that sometimes perceptions may not be true. We can carry with us perceptions of unforgiveness and resentment into all of our dealings. We keep piling each offense one on top of the other until we can't seem to see over them anymore. Our unforgiveness and resentment become the way we view all things.

Trust me on this one. I am much older and have done this very thing. I did not forgive each offense as it took place. Each offense, added to the next, creating a HUGE offense that threatened to choke me. Do you think the offenders lost sleep over my hurts? No. By my unwillingness to forgive I have given someone else power over my emotions and me. I know now that as I forgive, I am the one who benefits. I am released and can move on. I become what I am to be instead of being what has been done to me. In essence, I claim my own power back.

So, take that tool out! Be the bigger person! Don't give anyone power over you! Move on to bigger and better things . . . and always remember some "better" things are not things **at all!**

" . . . Wisdom perfects a person's speculative reason in matters of judgment about the truth." (Thomas Aquinas)

Tool Nine

" . . . Wisdom perfects a person's speculative reason in matters of judgement about the truth." (Thomas Aquinas)

This tool is really important. It is the *tool of Wisdom*. Hmm, how does one go about getting this one? Well, my young grasshopper, this one is received over time. We have put you on the path towards it and now the rest is up to you.

It will grow unbeknownst to you as you make each choice in your adult life. One day you will look back and see what you have gained from all of your experiences and choices. Every book you have read, every decision that you have made, every friend you have dropped or kept, every inspiring situation, every bad situation, and every love will help this tool grow. As you can see, the *tool of knowledge* and the *tool of love and passion* are very important in the development of this tool. Gaining the *knowledge* utilizing your *loves* and *passions* will enable *wisdom* to abound as you grow.

Wisdom is like paint color chosen for a home. The paint color brings out the structure of the house. Well, wisdom brings out how you have utilized a lot of the tools in your toolbox.

Remember over the next few decades to be patient with yourself and pull out all of your other handy dandy tools to work on this one! It will be well worth it in the end.

"If I only had courage."
(said the Cowardly Lion in the *Wizard of Oz*)

Tool Ten

"If I only had courage."
(said the Cowardly Lion in the *Wizard of Oz*)

Do you think the *tool of courage* is about screaming the loudest, shaking your fist the longest, or brandishing a sword or gun in a swash buckling adventure, Hollywood style?

The dictionary defines it as: "1. the quality of mind or spirit that enables a person to face difficulty, danger, pain, etc., without fear; bravery . . . ." Hmmm, kind of changes the image of the word, doesn't it? Courage is a noble tool that, believe it or not, just about everyone takes out and utilizes.

Courage comes in many forms. It comes in the form of a mother sacrificing food for her child. It comes in the form of a father staying up all night in a hospital to be by the side of a loved one. It comes in the form of anyone who gets up every single morning and gets ready for work. You can see it in the person living in a wheelchair as they adjust their lifestyle to accommodate it. You see it in family members as they grapple with getting a loved one off of drugs or alcohol. You can see it in the soldier who uses his body as a human shield to protect someone else. What about the person who stops at a car accident and helps the injured? What about you? Where do you fit in the tool of courage? When, as a teen struggling with the onslaught of peer pressure, did you ever take this tool out?

You did. Yes, I know, there were times where courage was not evident as you tried so hard to fit in. Let's examine this tool a little more closely. Did you help a friend in need? Did you hold that door open for the student in a wheel chair at school? Did you get up just about every morning and head off to school? Did you participate in this dance of life no matter how self-conscious you felt? Did you make it through?

The question "Did you make it through?" leads into the next tool learned.

"I think I can, I think I can"
('The Little Engine that Could')

Tool Eleven

"I think I can, I think I can."
(*"The Little Engine that Could"*)

Well, my dear, it is so hard to not share this tool with you. I remember when you were little exposing you to the book, "The little Engine That Could". Remember that little train engine? She just could not carry the full load over the mountain. What did she do? She went around asking for help. She started with the statelier of engines. (I think you know the type . . . they have the brains, the brawns and the resources!) All of these know—it-alls and have-it-alls turned the little engine away. Then, alas, she came across another little engine. She asked for help from this little engine and it readily agreed to help her in her time of need. And guess what? Between the two of them, they thought they could and did! No matter what the odds were that little engine was not going to be daunted at the task that was given to her. She rose to the occasion and found a way to get the job done . . . . She took out the ***tool of perseverance***. That little engine was willing to do whatever it took to make a difference and get the job done with dignity. She refused to give up. This tool will be taken out at all stages and seasons of your life, my friend.

As our journeys have been intertwined for many years, you have witnessed this tool being brought out time and time again when we were visited by the impossible. Remember those times? I sure do! At this moment they are faded painful memories of intense growth. I would not trade one season of turning, "I think I can't" to "I think I can" and then to "I thought I could".

Remember that old adage, "If the door closed to one opportunity, a window will open to another." The tool of perseverance will find that window of opportunity in the door closings of life.

I have witnessed your own seasons of door closings and have also witnessed windows opening up for you. The best advice I can give you is to not bang too long on the closed doors. Look for the open windows. They do come and they are there. Be that little engine that could; keep plugging, keep growing, and keep strong.

Which leads me to the last but not least . . . .

Step Three: Make a decision to turn our will and our lives over to the care of God as we understood Him.

Tool Twelve

Step Three: Make a decision to turn our will and our lives over to the care of God as we understood Him.

My child, as I said in the beginning of this love letter to you, you will always be my child no matter how old you are. It is one of the most awesome honors and privileges I have as your parent. You were conceived in the womb. I birthed you and watched you grow.

I had many sleepless nights of worry and tears. I worried about the daily decisions and the concern over my choices and how they would affect you. Some of the choices were out of my own control, yet they demanded a response from me, knowing that they would affect your heart and spirit. It was at those points in my life where I was brought to my knees. I would ask that God of ours to please fill the holes that my choice might leave behind.

I took out that ***tool of belief*** in my God as I understood Him. I love how the twelve step groups have expressed it in the third step. "Make a decision to turn our will and our lives over to the care of God as we understood Him."

There were times in my life where it seemed to be so dark for so long. I did not know which way to turn as I grappled and stumbled my way through seasons of heartache. I took your grandmother's unspoken advice as I watched her live her quiet, consistent life. I would go to bed and get up the next day walking through my life. I would go back to bed and get up and walk through next day and the next and the next. There were times where I never thought I would even make it through.

Looking back at those times, I know that it was the *tool of belief* in my God that propelled me to take up the *tool of love and passion*: a love of my God spread throughout my own heart and overflowed to you, my child. This love brought out the *tools of perseverance and courage.* The *tool of courage* was brought out to stand up tall inspite of circumstances and knowing that life was still going to go on. The *tool of perseverance* is what moved me to take out the *tool of knowledge*, to learn all that I could about the situation and about you and myself. The *tool of knowledge* brought me the *tool of listening* as I gained in understanding. As I gained in understanding the *tool of wisdom* was being sharpened. The *tool of wisdom* leads me to *the tool of forgiveness* which allowed me to let go of the hurts and move forward. Which, in turn, lead me full circle to taking out the *tool of a sense of humor* as I continued planning celebrations and dancing in my kitchen repeating to myself, "This too shall pass." Or better yet, remember the chocolates I would hide in my closet? I would go into my closet, take out my stash and while nibbling on a wonderful piece of chocolate I would say to myself, "I am special." It worked most of the time!

See how all are so intertwined, it all kind of works together somehow. You taught me that! You did! The power of the powerless is awesome! A mere child, what can a child accomplish? You don't pay taxes, you are not working full time nor providing for anyone. You are just being you! And in doing so, you have forever altered the course of my existence.

Thank you. Thank you for showing me how to develop my own toolbox. Thank you for teaching me the lessons of life as you developed one. Thank you for sharing your life with me. And since we are still on the tool of belief, thank you God for sharing my child's life with me.

I love you.

Further tidbits of wisdom

Always where underwear: Your clothes will last longer.

You cannot afford to buy cheap. You end up paying more in the end.

It is hardships that help us meet ourselves.

Read "Man's Search for Meaning". It will help you in your own search for meaning.

We do what we have to do to do what we want to do.

Never feel a job is too beneath you. Every job has a reason and a purpose. Some of the most menial jobs are the backbone that keeps everything else in place.

Construction workers, electricians, truck drivers and plumbers rule! They keep us in buildings, wired with light, full of merchandise and able to flush!

Life IS good because God says so.

Always keep in mind what you learned in preschool: play nice and when leaving your playground pick up after yourself.

You are always loved whether you know it or not.

When you think you can get away with something because no one can see you, remember, you are being watched. You just can't see God in body form.

Life IS good because God says so. Did I already say that?

What you see on the news are just snapshots of someone else's crisis/bad day. It is not the flow of real life.

The flow of real life is the door being held for an elderly person. It is the stopping to help someone change a flat tire. It is the wiping of tears from a small child as you reunite him/her with its parents. It is the giving of your clothing and furniture to someone who lost everything in a fire or flood. It is in the clasping of wrinkled, old and tired hands as it gives thanks for another day of wonder. It is in the success of a job well done. It is in the hands of everyone. It is in your hands.

As you lay your head down don't forget to thank the "Big Guy" for the day.

Embrace your bad day. You will have less of them.

Love those who can't stand you. It will drive them crazy.

Marry your best friend.

Make your word mean something.

People will remember more how you made them feel than what you said. Make them feel awesome.

Always shake hands firmly and look the person in the eye.

Read the Declaration of Independence AND the Constitution of the United States. It will change your life.

Edwards Brothers,Inc!
Thorofare, NJ 08086
01 Aug, 2010
BA2010213